MW00677689

FESTIVAL CRAFTS

By Chris Deshpande
Photographs by Zul Mukhida

Contents

Gareth Stevens Publishing
MILWAUKEE

About this book

What's your favorite day of the year? Perhaps it's your birthday or a festival day, such as Christmas, Kwanzaa, Chanukah, or Holi. This book is about festivals and how they are celebrated around the world. It shows you how to make craft projects associated with festivals and gives plenty of ideas to help you design your own.

This book will tell you about stories, traditions, and crafts that are based on festivals. At the back of the book, there is information on how to find out more about these crafts and traditions, with details about places to visit and books to read.

Some of the craft activities in this book are more complicated than others and will take longer to finish. It might be fun to ask some friends to help with these more difficult activities, such as making the Advent curiosity box on pages 26-27.

Before you start working on any of the craft projects, read through the instructions carefully. Most of the step-by-step instructions have a number. Look for the same number in the picture to see what each stage of your project should look like.

Before you begin

Collect everything listed in the "You will need" box or general project directions.

Ask an adult's permission if you are going to use a sharp tool, dye cloth, or use an oven.

Prepare a clear work surface.

If the activity is going to be messy, cover the surface with old newspaper or a waterproof sheet.

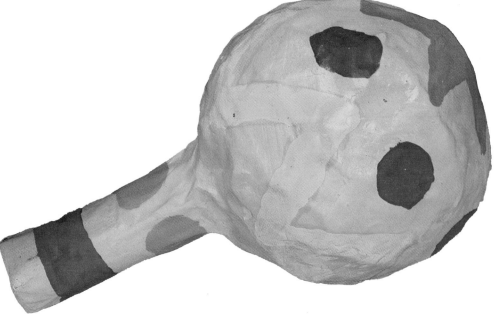

3

Mardi Gras

Mardi Gras is carnival time in many places. At the famous Mardi Gras carnival in Rio de Janeiro, Brazil, there are parties, feasts, and parades in the streets. These celebrations mark the beginning of Lent, which is the time when Christians remember the story of Jesus' fast in the wilderness.

Mardi Gras is also known as Fat Tuesday because people used to eat up any eggs, fat, and butter in the house before giving them up for Lent. In England, people eat pancakes, and the day is known as Pancake Day or Shrove Tuesday.

At Mardi Gras, there are colorful processions, with people having as much fun as possible before Lent. There is music, singing, and dancing; and people wear amazing masks and costumes.

Try to make a papier-mâché maraca to shake at carnival time. Maracas are made from hollow gourds filled with beads.

You will need:
- newspaper torn into pieces
- a small bowl of wallpaper paste without fungicide
- a large roll of clear tape
- a glue brush
- a balloon
- dried chickpeas
- paints
- paintbrushes
- varnish
- a piece of thin cardboard for the handle, about 3-1/2 inches (9 centimeters) square

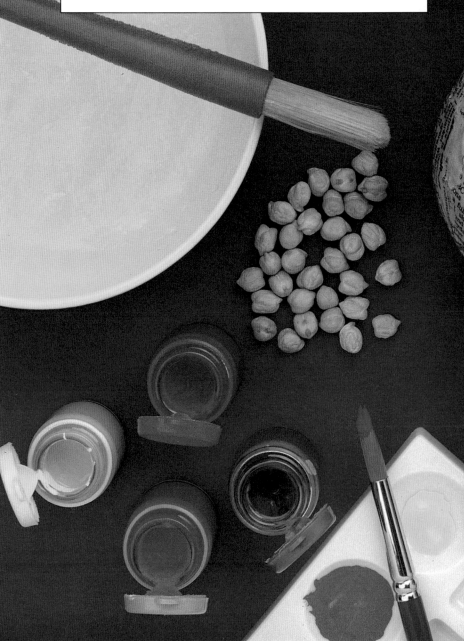

1 Blow up the balloon but don't make it too big. Rest the knotted end in the middle of a large roll of clear tape so it is easy to work on. Gently brush wallpaper paste all over the balloon. Dip a piece of paper into the paste and then place it on the balloon. Continue to cover the balloon with pasted paper, overlapping the pieces slightly to make a smooth surface. Cover the balloon with about four layers of paper.

2 To make the handle, roll the cardboard into a narrow tube and tape the ends together. Attach the handle to the balloon by pasting long strips of paper to the handle and halfway up the balloon. Strengthen the joint around the neck of the balloon with strips of paper that run the other way. Cover the balloon with paste and let it dry for about two days.

3 Pop the balloon with a needle. Put a handful of chickpeas into the hollow maraca. Block up the handle with some scrunched-up newspaper. Cover with papier-mâché to seal the end. Let it dry. Paint and varnish your maraca.

5

Easter

Easter is a Christian festival that is celebrated around the world. It recalls the story of Jesus' return from the dead. Christians believe Jesus died on the cross on Good Friday. In Germany, this day is known as Silent Friday because no church bells are rung. On Easter Sunday, Christians believe Jesus rose from the dead.

The word Easter *comes from the name of the ancient goddess of spring, who was called "Eostre." Many Easter customs are based on the springtime flowering of plants and birth of animals. Often at Easter, chocolate and decorated eggs are given as presents because eggs are a symbol of new life.*

Here are some ways to decorate hard-boiled eggs. Try to make up some of your own as well. **Ask an adult to help you hard-boil the eggs.** Make sure the eggs are cold before you start to decorate them.

In Poland, wax designs are painted on eggs. This kind of design is called batik. Try making your own batik eggs.

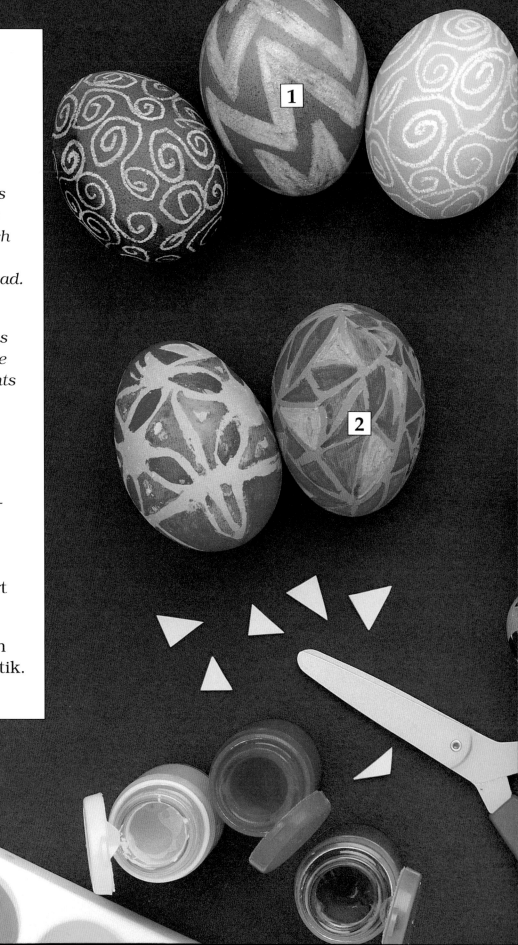

1 Draw your design on a hard-boiled egg with a wax crayon. Place the egg in a bowl of vegetable dye, made from either cold tea or the water left over from cooking spinach or beets. Or you can mix 1 tablespoon (15 milliliters) of turmeric with a cup of hot water. Leave the egg in the dye for thirty minutes.

2 Draw a pattern with wax crayon onto a hard-boiled egg and color the spaces in between with poster paint.

3 Cut shapes from tissue paper and paste onto an egg with white glue.

4 Eggs can be painted with poster paint or inks. You can also decorate them with colored paper.

5 Carefully drain a hard-boiled egg on a slotted spoon. While the egg is still hot, pick it up with a towel. Mark up the entire egg with a wax crayon. The heat of the egg melts the crayon and makes a smooth coating of wax. When the egg is cool, scratch a design into the wax coating with a toothpick.

Eid ul-Fitr

Eid ul-Fitr is an important festival in the Islamic calendar that comes at the end of a month-long fast called Ramadan. During Ramadan, Muslims do not eat or drink anything from dawn until after sunset.

Eid ul-Fitr is a happy time when people go to parties, buy new clothes, and give each other presents and cards. The Muslim religion forbids the drawing of people or animals, so Eid ul-Fitr cards are decorated with beautiful designs made from geometric patterns.

Try designing your own geometric patterns and printing your own cards or wrapping paper. To find some ideas for your patterns, look at pictures of Islamic buildings, such as the Dome of the Rock in Jerusalem, below.

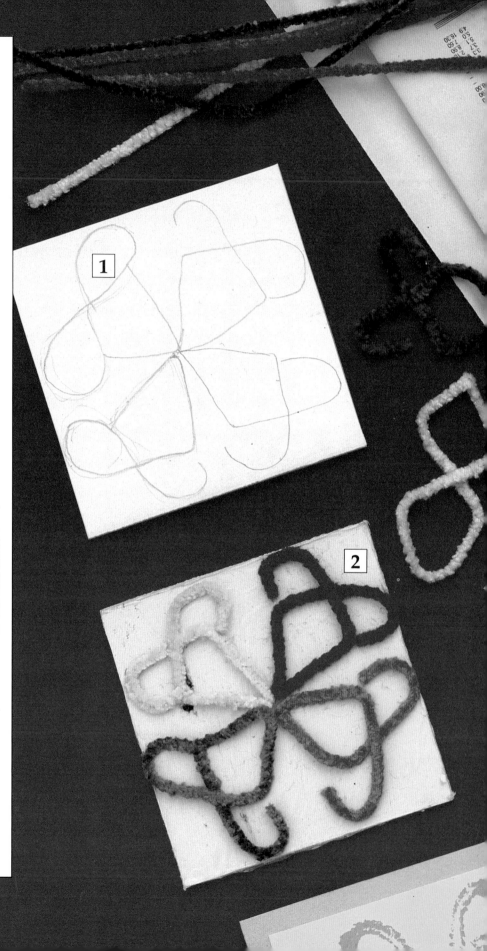

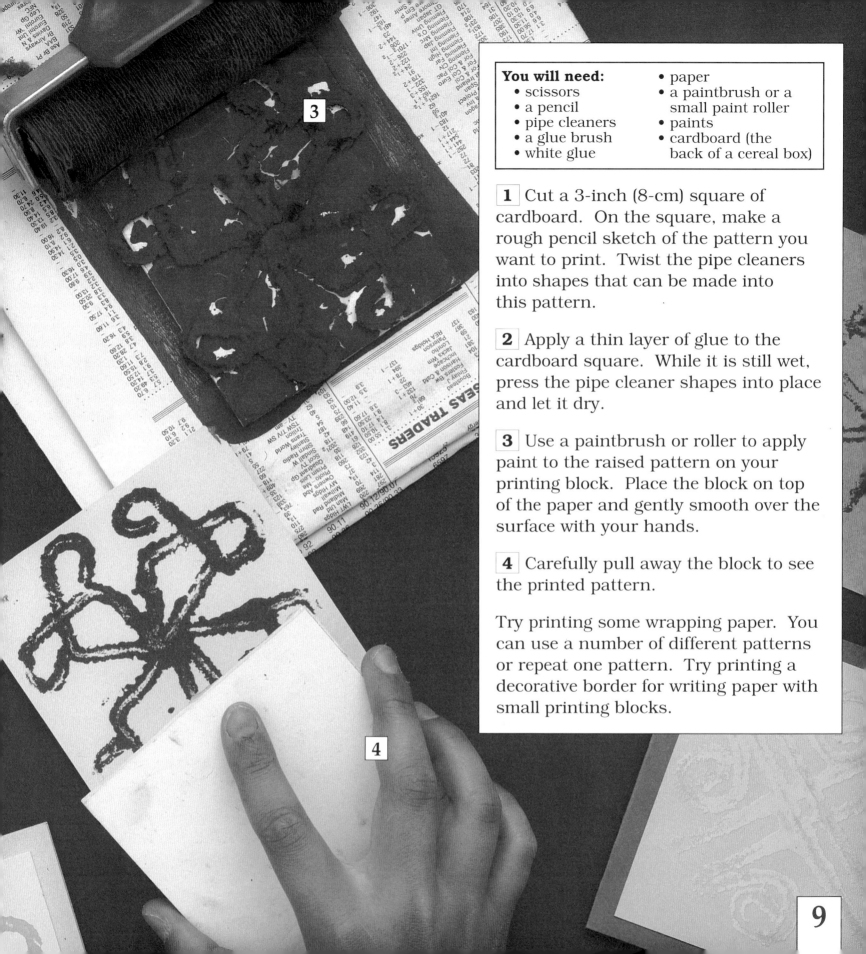

3

4

1 Cut a 3-inch (8-cm) square of cardboard. On the square, make a rough pencil sketch of the pattern you want to print. Twist the pipe cleaners into shapes that can be made into this pattern.

2 Apply a thin layer of glue to the cardboard square. While it is still wet, press the pipe cleaner shapes into place and let it dry.

3 Use a paintbrush or roller to apply paint to the raised pattern on your printing block. Place the block on top of the paper and gently smooth over the surface with your hands.

4 Carefully pull away the block to see the printed pattern.

Try printing some wrapping paper. You can use a number of different patterns or repeat one pattern. Try printing a decorative border for writing paper with small printing blocks.

9

Holi

Holi is a Hindu festival held in the spring. It is celebrated mostly in India. Holi is a time of games and pranks when people remember the stories of Lord Krishna and the tricks and jokes he played. There are processions for three to five days, and people sing and dance in the streets.

Make a splatter painting

You will need:
- old newspaper
- an old sponge
- water
- paints
- paintbrushes
- paper

Splatter painting can be messy, so before you begin put down lots of old newspaper. Use the sponge to dampen a clean sheet of paper but be careful not to make the paper too wet. Use a paintbrush to flick and drip paint onto the paper, or take a pinch of powder paint and drop it onto the paper. Watch the patterns form as the paint runs.

1

Holi is also a festival that celebrates the arrival of spring and the blossoming of spring flowers.

Make a paper flower garland

You will need:
- scissors
- thread
- stem wire
- a roll of crêpe paper
- a big needle

1 To make one flower, cut a 3-inch (8-cm)-wide strip from the folded roll of crêpe paper.

2 Unroll this strip and roll it up again loosely into a cylinder shape, crunching the paper as you go. Wrap wire around the middle of the paper. Tuck in any sharp pieces of wire or cover them with tape.

3 On either side of the wire, open out the crêpe paper into petals. Make lots of flowers in this way.

4 To make a garland, use a big needle and thread to sew the flowers together.

Look at different flowers and see if you can make paper ones that look similar. Try to make paper daffodils and roses.

The Dragon Boat Festival

At the Chinese Dragon Boat Festival, races are held in brightly colored boats that are decorated with dragons' heads and tails. Everybody makes a lot of noise and splashes the water.

Many people believe the festival is based on the story of a poet called Qu Yuan, who lived in ancient China. Qu Yuan thought the rulers of his day were cruel and unfair, so he decided to drown himself in protest. He threw himself into the middle of the river. All the villagers raced their boats across the river to try to save Qu Yuan, but they were too late. The poet drowned. The villagers were worried that the fish in the lake would disturb the poet's body, so they made lots of noise to frighten the fish away.

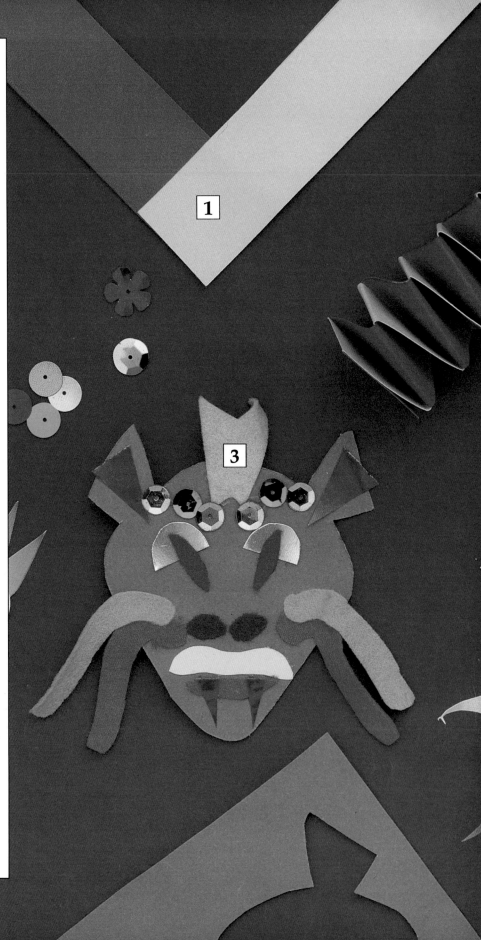

1

3

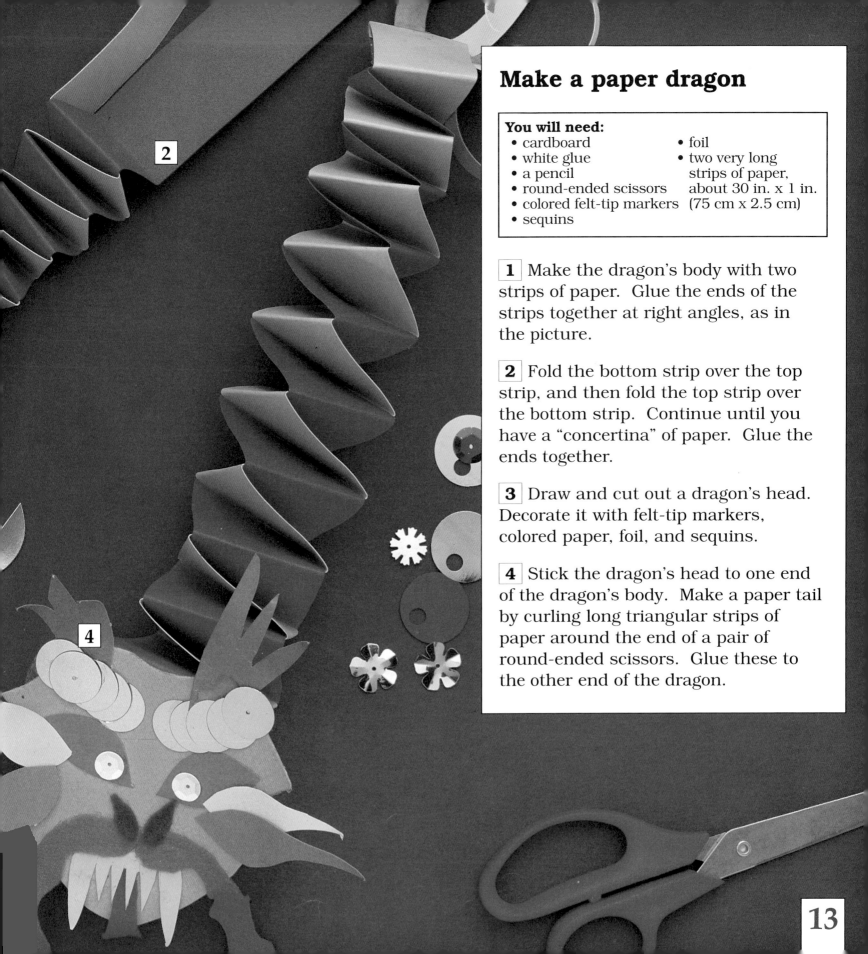

Make a paper dragon

You will need:
- cardboard
- white glue
- a pencil
- round-ended scissors
- colored felt-tip markers
- sequins
- foil
- two very long strips of paper, about 30 in. x 1 in. (75 cm x 2.5 cm)

1 Make the dragon's body with two strips of paper. Glue the ends of the strips together at right angles, as in the picture.

2 Fold the bottom strip over the top strip, and then fold the top strip over the bottom strip. Continue until you have a "concertina" of paper. Glue the ends together.

3 Draw and cut out a dragon's head. Decorate it with felt-tip markers, colored paper, foil, and sequins.

4 Stick the dragon's head to one end of the dragon's body. Make a paper tail by curling long triangular strips of paper around the end of a pair of round-ended scissors. Glue these to the other end of the dragon.

Raksha Bandhan

Raksha Bandhan is a festival celebrated by most Hindu and Sikh families. It's a day when families remind each other how much they love one another. On this day, a sister ties a plaited bracelet, called a rakhi, around her brother's wrist, and he promises to look after her.

There are many stories about Raksha Bandhan. Here is a Hindu story. Indra, who was the King of the Gods, lost his heavenly kingdom in a war with the demon King Bali. Indra's wife prayed for help. Then Lord Vishnu gave her an amulet, or lucky charm, which he told her to tie around Indra's wrist. The amulet protected Indra in battle, and good triumphed over evil.

You can make plaited rakhis from long strips of fabric, string, ribbon, or wool. You will need strips of fabric or thread that are roughly two-and-a-half times the length of the plait you want to make. Here's how to make a three-strand rakhi with ribbon.

Knot the ends of the ribbon together. It may help to pin the ribbon to a cork board. Move the threads over each other as shown. When you have moved each ribbon once, repeat the moves. To finish the plait, knot the ends of the ribbon together.

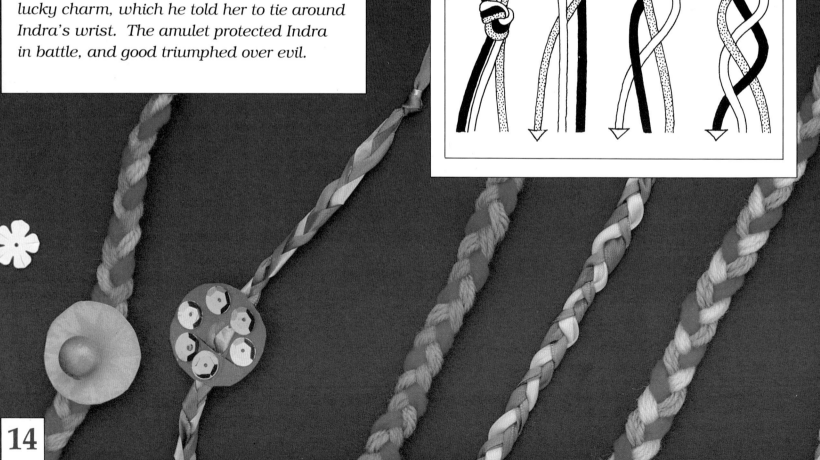

Try making a five-strand rakhi from thick wool. This plait is made in two steps that are repeated. It will help if you use five different colored wools.

Knot the ends of the wool together. First, the far right thread is taken over the next two threads to the center. Then the far left thread goes over the next two threads, to the center. After five steps, the order of the threads is reversed. After ten steps, the threads are back in place. To finish, knot the ends of the threads together.

Decorate a small circle of cardboard with foil and sequins. Sew the decorated circle to the middle of the plaited band. You can give your rakhi to a family member or a friend.

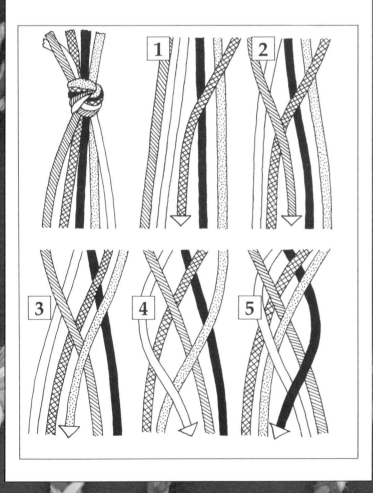

Harvest

People celebrate the gathering of the harvest all over the world. After the hard work of planting and tending to the crops all year, harvest is a time of happiness and thanksgiving.

In Punjab in India, villagers perform a very energetic dance called Bhangra, which acts out the sowing, tending, and reaping of the crops.

Long ago in England, the last of the corn harvest was set aside, ground, and twisted into the shape of a person, a sheaf of wheat, or a cross. These shapes became known as corn dollies. The dolly was kept through the winter and sown with new corn the next spring. The corn spirit was then "saved and kept alive" until the following spring.

Make some harvest models from salt dough

You will need:
- 1-1/2 cups (325 grams) plain flour
- 1 cup (225 g) salt
- 1 cup (250 ml) water
- 1 tablespoon (15 ml) oil
- a wooden spoon
- greaseproof paper
- food coloring
- a bowl
- paints
- varnish
- paintbrush
- a cookie sheet
- an oven set to 300°F (150°C)

Mix the flour and salt together. Then add the water and oil. Shake some flour over your hands and knead the mixture into a dough.

Use a small piece of dough and model it into the shape of a harvest corn dolly. Try making models of your favorite harvest fruits and vegetables.

You can color the salt dough with food coloring before you cook it. Add a few drops of coloring to the dough. Knead in the color to make it even. Or you can cook your salt dough shape first and then paint and varnish it afterward.

Put your models onto a cookie sheet lined with greaseproof paper. **Ask an adult to help you put it in the oven.** Bake for about one hour and fifteen minutes, until the models are hard.

Chanukah

Chanukah is the Jewish festival of light. It is based on the following ancient story. A Syrian emperor forbade the Jews from praying in their temple in Jerusalem. The Jews eventually won back the temple, but there was only enough oil for the eternal light for one day. Miraculously, the oil lasted eight days. This is why Chanukah lasts for eight days.

The Chanukiyah is a candlestick with nine holders. It holds a candle for each day of the festival and a servant candle that is used to light the others. The Chanukiyah stands for light, truth, and the triumph of good over evil.

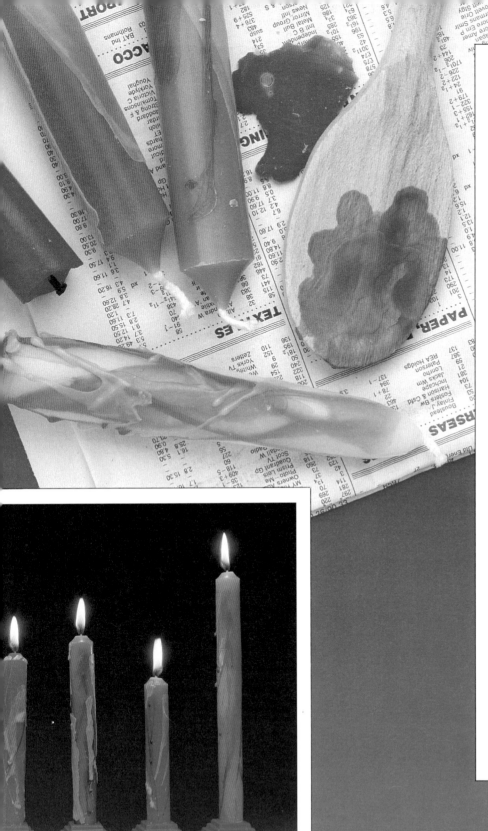

The oldest Jewish symbol is a seven-branched candlestick called a menorah. Each branch symbolizes one of the days of creation.

Decorate a candle

You will need:
- a kettle
- a long candle
- a hot plate or stove
- a wooden spoon
- a small saucepan
- an empty, shallow tin can
- the stub from an old, colored, non-flammable wax candle
- an old wooden chopping board or cork mat resting on plenty of newspaper

Ask an adult to help you prepare the hot wax. Put the stub of an old colored candle into the can. Stand the can in the saucepan. Boil some water in the kettle and pour about 1-1/2 inches (4 cm) into the bottom of the saucepan. Gently heat the saucepan until the wax melts.

Ask an adult to help you remove the saucepan from the heat. Place the saucepan on a wooden chopping board.

Hold the unused candle over the can and use the spoon to dribble colored wax over it. Allow the wax to harden.

Birthdays

What special things do you do on your birthday to remember the day on which you were born? All over the world, people celebrate birthdays with parties and presents. In South America, children are given "God's Eyes" on their birthdays. These are sticks fastened into a cross and woven with colored wool. Each different color of wool stands for a year of the child's life.

You can make tiny God's Eyes from toothpicks or bigger ones from bamboo canes and craft sticks.

You will need:
- heavy cotton thread
- scissors
- white glue
- toothpicks or longer craft sticks
- beads
- lengths of different colored wool or strips of fabric

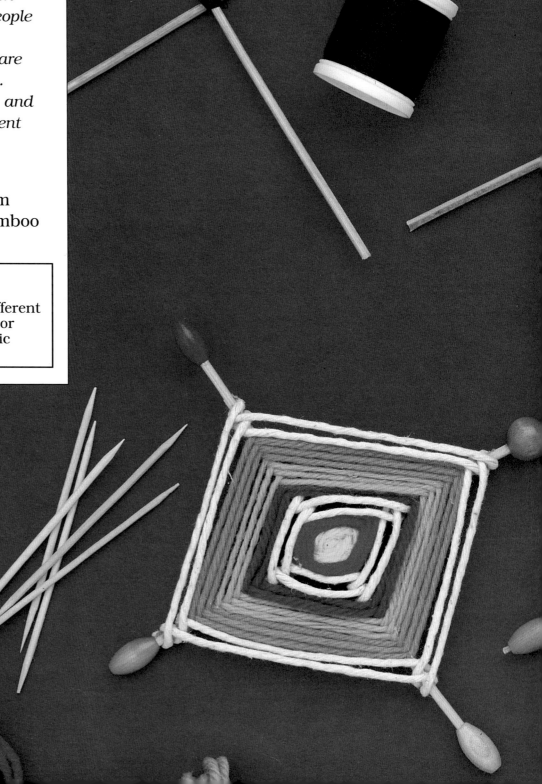

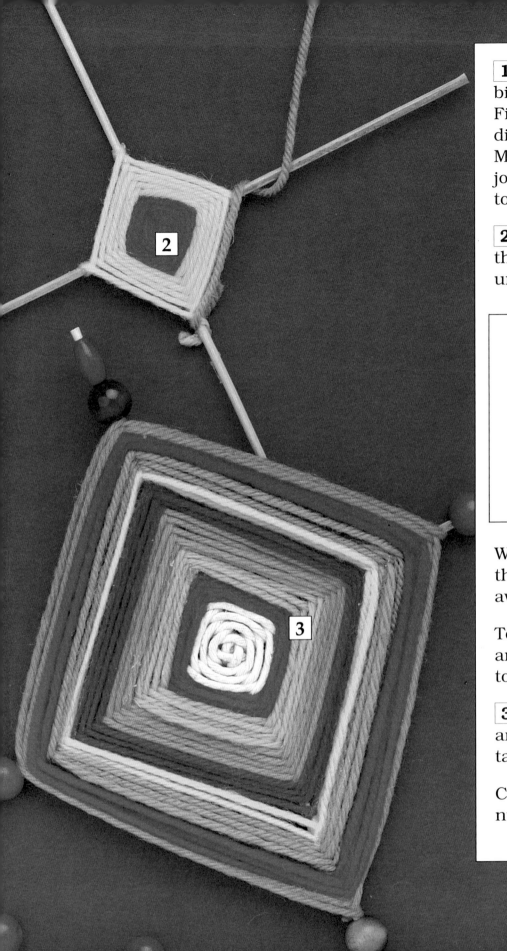

1 Find the middles of two sticks and bind them together with cotton thread. First, wrap the thread around the sticks diagonally one way, and then the other. Make sure the sticks are securely joined. Tie the two ends of the thread together and cut just beneath the knot.

2 Glue the end of one length of wool to the center. Wrap the wool over and under each arm in turn, as pictured.

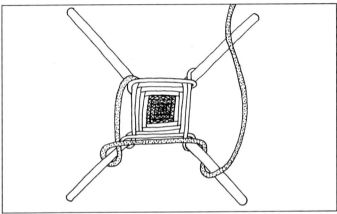

When you want to finish one color, glue the wool firmly around one arm and cut away any spare wool.

To start a new color, glue the wool around this same arm. Then continue to wrap the wool in a figure eight.

3 Try gluing beads on the ends of the arms of your God's Eyes. Or make tassels that hang from the arms.

Can you think of a way of joining a number of God's Eyes together?

All Souls' Day

All Souls' Day is a day when the Christian Church remembers people who have died. Some people believe that on the night of All Souls' Day (November 2) the souls, or spirits, of dead people visit their former homes. Some people place lanterns and candles in their windows to guide the spirits to food and drink that has been prepared for them inside. In Mexico, some families make an altar in their homes for dead relatives. They decorate the altar with marigolds and sugar-icing skulls.

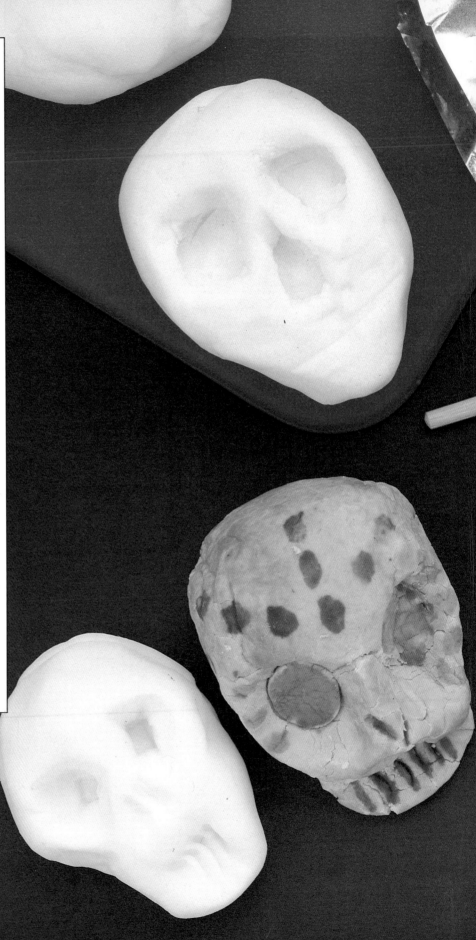

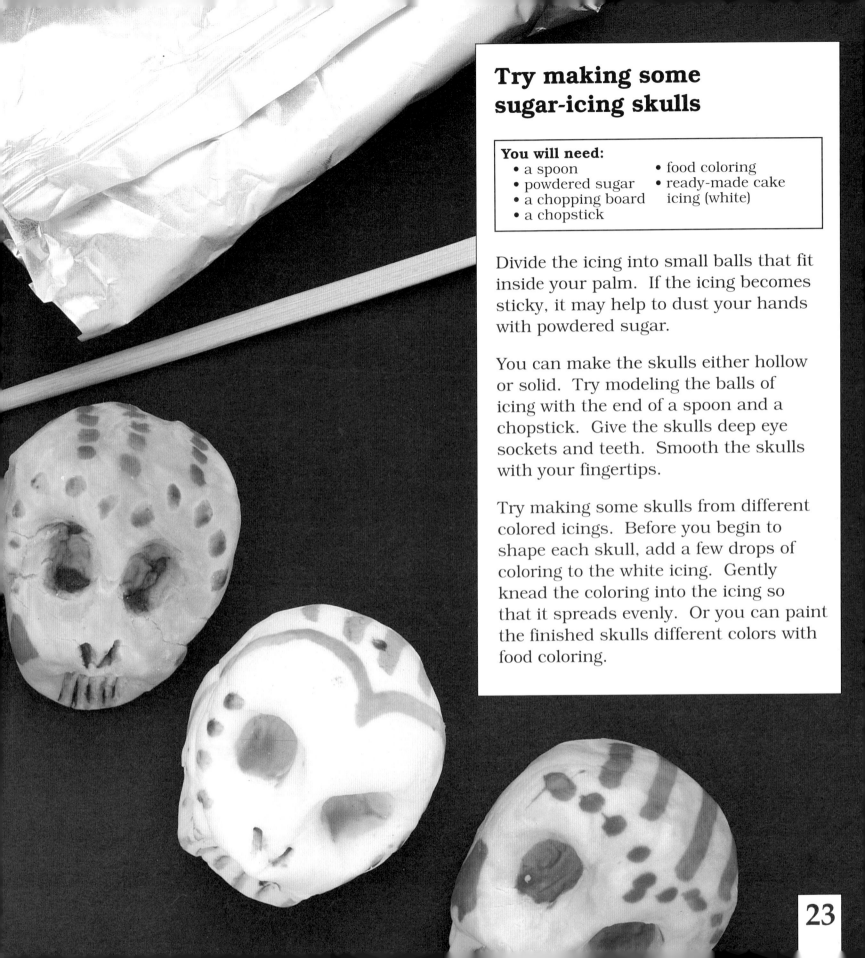

Try making some sugar-icing skulls

You will need:
- a spoon
- powdered sugar
- a chopping board
- a chopstick
- food coloring
- ready-made cake icing (white)

Divide the icing into small balls that fit inside your palm. If the icing becomes sticky, it may help to dust your hands with powdered sugar.

You can make the skulls either hollow or solid. Try modeling the balls of icing with the end of a spoon and a chopstick. Give the skulls deep eye sockets and teeth. Smooth the skulls with your fingertips.

Try making some skulls from different colored icings. Before you begin to shape each skull, add a few drops of coloring to the white icing. Gently knead the coloring into the icing so that it spreads evenly. Or you can paint the finished skulls different colors with food coloring.

Kwanzaa

Kwanzaa is an African-American harvest festival that also celebrates the values of traditional African customs. Kwanzaa was first observed in 1966 and is now celebrated each year from December 26 through January 1.

Seven candles are lit during the Kwanzaa celebration to represent traditional African principles. A Swahili word is used to name each of these values. For example, kuumba means "creativity," and umoja means "unity."

Family members give simple gifts, known as zawadi, to one another during the Kwanzaa celebration. These gifts are often handcrafted items, such as necklaces or other jewelry. This jewelry is worn with other traditional African clothing.

Try making a zawadi necklace

You will need:
- heavy cotton thread or cord at least 2 feet (60 cm) long
- self-hardening clay or salt dough (see page 17)
- a darning needle
- wooden or ceramic beads
- a toothpick
- thick, coated wire
- scissors

Make a flattened disk approximately 1/2-inch (1.2-cm) thick and 1-1/2 inch (4 cm) in diameter out of self-hardening clay or salt dough. Carefully poke the wire through the top of the disk to make an opening into which you can insert the cord or thread.

Use a toothpick or pencil to score a design on one side of the disk. You may want to make a geometric design or represent a plant or animal that is native to Africa. Let the disk dry completely.

Thread the darning needle with thick cotton cord or thread, and knot one end. String the beads onto the cord or thread, alternating colors as desired.

When you reach the middle of the length of cord, add your handcrafted disk so that it is positioned in the center of the strand.

Continue adding beads on the other side of the disk until your necklace is complete. Carefully knot the cord or thread and trim the ends.

You may wish to present your necklace to a family member or friend as a zawadi during Kwanzaa.

Christmas

Christmas is the time when the Christian Church celebrates the story of the birth of Jesus. The month leading up to Christmas is known as Advent, which means the "coming." Some churches have Advent wreaths, which are circles of woven holly, with holders for four candles. Holly, which is evergreen, symbolizes new life, and the candles symbolize Jesus as the light of the world. On each Sunday leading up to Christmas, a candle is lit. This custom comes from Scandinavia.

Advent calendars are often given to children as presents. The calendars have twenty-five windows that open out to show pictures. A window is opened on each day leading up to Christmas. The last window is opened on Christmas morning.

Advent calendars are fun and easy to make. Try to make one that can hold small presents.

> **You will need:**
> - elastic bands
> - cardboard
> - scissors
> - sequins
> - felt-tip pens
> - paints
> - a paintbrush
> - white glue
> - 25 paper fasteners
> - colored paper
> - 25 empty matchboxes that are all the same size

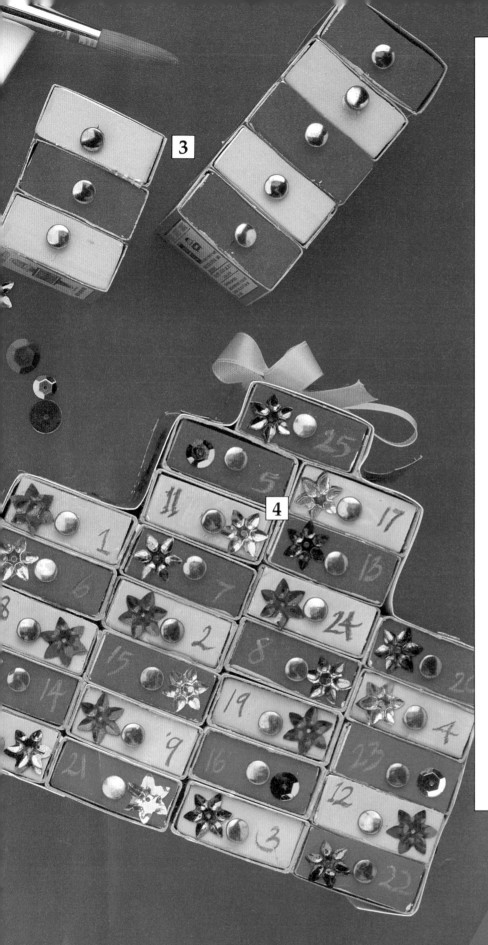

1 Paint the drawers of the boxes. For the handles, make a hole in the middle of the front of each drawer and push in a paper fastener. Open out the arms of the paper fasteners at the back to hold them in place.

Put each drawer back in its shell.

2 Before you glue your boxes into columns, think about how you want your Advent calendar to look. Each column could be the same height, or you can make an Advent calendar with columns of different heights, similar to the one in the picture. When you've decided, glue the boxes on top of each other. To help the boxes stay in place while they dry, place a rubber band around them.

3 When each column has dried, glue the columns next to each other. Number the drawers from one to twenty-five.

4 Cut the cardboard to cover the top and sides of the big box and glue on.

Decorate your Advent box with paper shapes and sequins.

Make tiny presents to put inside each box. What will you put inside box number twenty-five, which is opened on Christmas morning?

New Year

Many religions have their own calendars, which means that people celebrate New Year at different times. The Sikhs celebrate their New Year, Baisaikhi, in April. The Hindus celebrate their New Year, Diwali, in late October or early November. The Jewish New Year festival called Rosh Hashanah happens in September or October.

In some parts of the world, New Year's Day is always on January 1. But many people use lunar calendars, which are arranged according to the phases of the moon, so New Year's Day changes its date each year.

Each New Year festival has its own traditions and customs. The Chinese name each year after one of twelve different animals. To celebrate the New Year, they make huge dancing dragons and decorate the streets with lanterns.

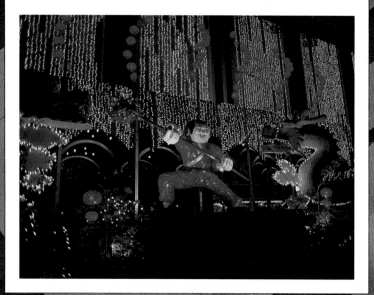

Try making some paper lanterns with paper that has been folded, cut, and scored into interesting patterns. Here are a few suggestions for ways to cut your paper. Try to make up some of your own as well.

You will need:
- cotton thread
- paper
- a pencil
- round-ended scissors
- transparent tape
- a ruler
- a flat work surface covered with lots of newspaper
- a craft knife

Ask an adult to help you use the craft knife.

1 Cut long triangular and rectangular strips from one or more sheets of paper. Gently curl them around a pair of round-ended scissors.

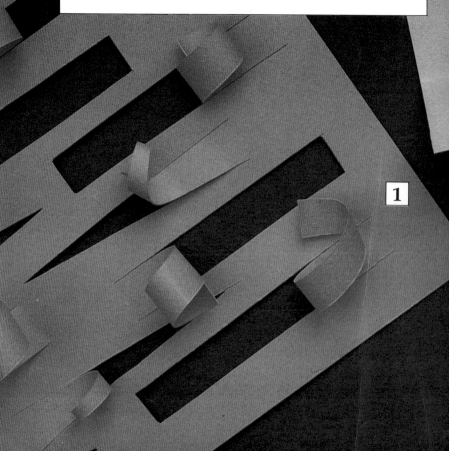

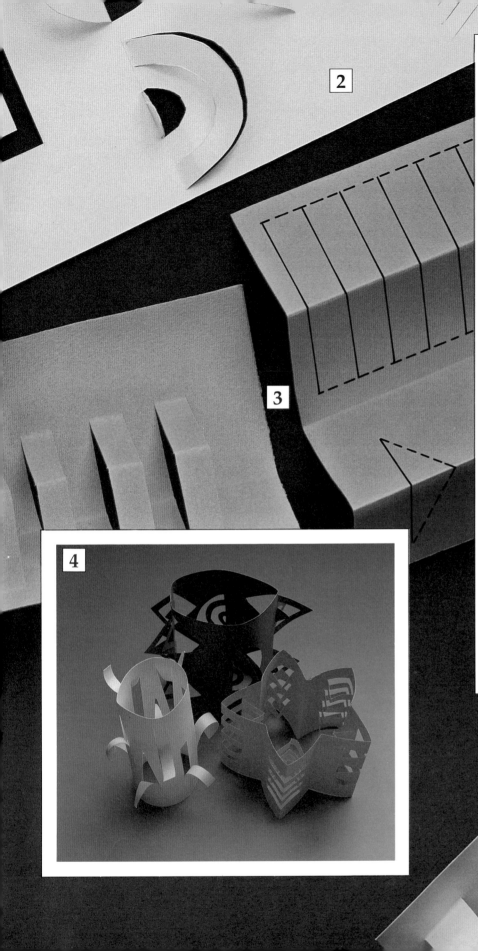

2 On another sheet of paper, draw an even number of half shapes that fit inside each other. Carefully cut around each line. Fold back every other strip of paper. Experiment with triangles, circles, and squares.

3 Take another piece of paper and fold or pleat it a few times. Press each fold firmly.

Use a ruler to draw squares, rectangles, and triangles on the center of each fold. Draw solid lines that run up and down the sides of the shapes. Draw dots for lines at the top and bottom of each shape.

Put a ruler on the dotted lines and score along them with a craft knife. Use the knife and ruler to cut along the solid lines. Push out the shapes from the fold.

4 When you have made cut-outs all over your piece of paper, stick the sides of the paper together to make a lantern. Attach some thread to the top of the lantern. Hang it by a window so light can shine through it.

More things to think about

This book shows you how to make and model papier-mâché and salt dough, cut and fold paper, and plait thread. You can use these different craft techniques to make your own craft items based on festivals.

Many festival days are a time of remembering happy or sad events or old stories. Sometimes the stories are religious. To get some ideas for making your own crafts, find out as much as you can about the story behind a festival.

As you find out more about a particular story, you will see that certain signs and symbols have come to stand for the festival; for example, dyed eggs at Easter. Some festivals share similar symbols, such as light, or the growth of plants and the birth of animals in spring. Can you think of your own symbols for certain festivals? Think about how you can use festival symbols in your craft designs.

Visit museums and ask older people in the community how festivals were celebrated in the past. Make sketches of any interesting decorations or symbols. Two hundred years ago, Christmas was celebrated very differently from the way it is celebrated today. Try to find out when Christmas trees first became popular.

Think of all the different ways that festivals can be celebrated. There may be parties where people wear traditional clothes and eat specially prepared food. Do you and your family have any special customs for festival days? Can you include any of these ideas in your craft project?

Find out how people in different parts of the world celebrate the same festival; for example, the harvest festival. Try to find out about harvest customs, traditions, and legends in the United States, China, India, and Italy.

Your craft project can be a decoration, greeting card, or a musical instrument. Think about the best craft technique to use. For example, you can model salt dough or papier-mâché, or cut and fold paper. Do you want the finished item to be flat or three-dimensional? Do you want it to have moving parts or to hang from the wall? When you have answered these and similar questions, think carefully about the best way of making your craft project and the best materials to use.

Experiment with different kinds of decoration for your craft project. How could you include symbols as decoration? Think about all the ways you can create different textures, colors, and shades using paper, cloth, or papier-mâché. Try making one huge and one tiny version of your project. For example, you can make an Advent calendar with matchboxes, or you can make an enormous Advent curiosity box.

For more information

More books to read

Adventures in Art
Susan Milford (Williamson)

Easter
Gail Gibbons (Holiday)

Festivals Around the World
Philip Steele (Dillon)

Fun with Paint
Moira Butterfield (Random House)

Hands Around the World
Susan Milford (Williamson)

Holidays Around the World
(Bantam)

Kids Explore America's African-American Heritage
Westridge Young Writers Workshop
(Jefferson School District No. R-1)

The Kids Multicultural Art Book
Alexandra M. Terzian (Williamson)

Magical Tales from Many Lands
Margaret Mayo
(Dutton's Children's Books)

Making Prints
Deri Robins (Kingfisher)

Paint
Kim Solga (North Light)

Piñatas and Paper Flowers
Lila Perl (Clarion)

60 Art Projects for Children
Jeannette M. Baumgardner
(Clarkson Potter)

Videos

Africa: Land and People (Barr Films)

Don't Eat the Pictures
Children's Television Workshop

Look What I Made: Paper Playthings and Gifts

My First Activity Video (Sony)

Places to visit

The following places have major collections of crafts from around the world. Don't forget to look in your area museum, too.

Canadian Museum of Civilization
100 Laurier Street
P.O. Box 3100, Station B
Hull, Quebec
J8X 4H2

Denver Museum of Natural History
2001 Colorado Boulevard
Denver, Colorado 80205

Franklin Institute
20th Street and the Franklin Parkway
Philadelphia, Pennsylvania 19103-1194

Royal British Columbia Museum
675 Belleville Street
Victoria, British Columbia
V8V 1X4

The Smithsonian Institution
1000 Jefferson Drive SW
Washington, D.C. 20560

Index

For a free color catalog describing
Gareth Stevens' list of high-quality
books, call 1-800-542-2595 (USA) or
1-800-461-9120 (Canada).
Gareth Stevens' Fax: (414) 225-0377.

**Library of Congress
Cataloging-in-Publication Data**
Deshpande, Chris.
    Festival crafts/Chris Deshpande; photographs
by Zul Mukhida.
    North American ed.
        p.   cm. — (Worldwide crafts)
    Includes bibliographical references and index.
    ISBN 0-8368-1153-4
    1. Handicraft—Juvenile literature. 2. Fasts
and feasts—Juvenile literature. [1. Handicraft.
2. Fasts and feasts.] I. Mukhida, Zul, ill. II.
Title. III. Series.
TT160.D38   1994
745.594'1—dc20   94-11431

North American edition first published
in 1994 by
Gareth Stevens Publishing
1555 North RiverCenter Drive, Suite 201
Milwaukee, Wisconsin 53212, USA

First published in 1993 by A & C Black
(Publishers) Limited, London; © 1993
A & C Black (Publishers) Limited.

Acknowledgments
Line drawings by Barbara Pegg. Photographs
by Zul Mukhida, except for: p. 4, p. 8, p. 28
Life File Photographic Agency; p. 12 Robert
Harding Photographic Agency; p. 18 Jewish
Education Bureau; pp. 24-25 Quad/Photo.

Grateful thanks to Langford and Hill, Ltd.,
London, for supplying all art materials.

Crafts made by Tracy Brunt except for those
on pp. 6-7, which were made by Dorothy Moir.